GASTON
Goes to Mardi Gras
COLORING BOOK

GASTON
Goes to Mardi Gras
COLORING BOOK

**Written and Illustrated
by James Rice**

**The Illustrator of
CAJUN NIGHT BEFORE CHRISTMAS**

PELICAN PUBLISHING COMPANY
GRETNA 2007

Printed in the United States
Published by Pelican Publishing Company, Inc.
1000 Burmaster Street, Gretna, Louisiana 70053

GASTON GOES TO MARDI GRAS

One day, Gaston saw a poster announcing the Mardi Gras in New Orleans. He decided to go to the city.

On the way he joined a *Courir du Mardi Gras* group.

The gumbo feast was followed by a *fais-do-do* that lasted till dawn.

Just across the Mississippi River from New Orleans, Gaston peeked in the window of a "den" where floats were being built.

There were parades every day, reaching a high point on Mardi
Gras, or Fat Tuesday.

Gaston liked the black Krewe of Zulu. He rocked to the Dixieland beat.

Floats passed one after the other. "Throw me something, Mister!" sounded from the sidelines.

The Jefferson City Buzzards, the oldest marching group in the city, were followed by a jazz band.

Boeuf Gras, or Fat Beef, the ancient symbol of Mardi Gras, passed.

Rex's parade stopped twice en route; once to toast the mayor and once to toast the queen.

More parades followed Rex, but few approached the mighty Rex in terms of lavish display.

The parades and floats continued into the night.

Rex and his court ruled over lavish balls. Carnival ended at the stroke of midnight.

Mardi Gras was many things, but most of all it was having fun!